MAELSTROM

the Four Scrolls of an Illyrian Sage

A Poem by

FAHREDIN SHEHU

2012
Prishtina
Kosovo

inner child press, ltd.

General Information

Maelstrom
the Four Scrolls of an Illyrian Sage

Fahredin Shehu

1st Edition : 2014

This Publishing is protected under Copyright Law as a "Collection". All rights for all submissions are retained by the Individual Author and or Artist. No part of this Publishing may be Reproduced, Transferred in any manner without the prior **WRITTEN CONSENT** of the "Material Owner" or it's Representative Inner Child Press. Any such violation infringes upon the Creative and Intellectual Property of the Owner pursuant to International and Federal Copyright Law. Any queries pertaining to this "Collection" should be addressed to Publisher of Record.

Publisher Information
1st Edition : Inner Child Press
innerchildpress@gmail.com
www.innerchildpress.com

This Collection is protected under U.S. and International Copyright Laws

Copyright © 2014 : Fahredin Shehu
LOC : 1-1203118911

ISBN-13 : 978-0615967424 (Inner Child Press, Ltd.)
ISBN-10 : 0615967426

$ 19.95

Dedication

To my daughter Tamara and my son Reis who are taught to be disgusted by the indifference of Mankind who passively observe the shameful extermination of the Iraqi Mandeans, by the extremists of all sorts in our age?

I imply all my Being in teaching them to love all and fear the malice facing due their future struggle for spreading Love.

Fahredin Shehu

September 2012
Prishtina
Kosovo

Acknowledgements

To all visible, semi-visible and invisible forces that surrounded and submitted to the grand will of the God Alone, who supported the accomplishment and materialization of this Theurgy.

To all receptive human who polished their hearts so the miracle of this Word may shine and warm the cold heart of the Mankind.

To all who disregard divisions, separations and prejudice on the origin of the Author, his mistakes and sins for he strived to bring forth The Ancient, The Present and The Future of the Word that embraces Creation and nothing is alien, creating the thread of prosperity of the Mankind.

I or better said we (or even better, the all "I"-s of the manifested in Author's name) is/are prostrated as it belongs to the real servants of the Mankind- to the Grand Master of the Universe i.e. LOVE.

My special thanks go to the incredible Humans from which I have absorbed the sparkling of their Souls in the gloomiest days of my existence and the dark nights stretching fear as wings of Bat.

To: Knut Ødegård (Norway), Milan Richter (Slovakia), Marek Wawrskievicz (Poland), Maria Alicia Bernal Philippines, Adrian Grima (Malta), Zeilton Feitosa (Brasil), Andre Cruchaga (Chile), Guiseppe Goffredo and Beppe Costa (Italy), Joan Manresa (Spain), Naim Aradi and Hava Pinhas Cohen (Israel), Gene Berry (Ireland), Abed Chehab (Lebanon), Ali Caglar and Omar Dincsoy (Turkey), Hadaa Sendoo and G Mend Ooyo (Mongolia), Arup K Chatterjee (India), Philip Larrimore and William S. Peters (USA) etc.

a few words from the Author

Every epoch had its "Word" yet it was emphasized, sometimes repeated combustive to shake the dormant Man we all bear as a sleeping Giant of Creativity.

Excluding nothing Human as alien- embracing all as part of the Body, recognition of Vision, Hearing and Perception, pondering on each tiny incident in Life until focusing on one point of concentration, creates a blend of "Word", that touches the most sensible Souls and the most distant Galaxies of the heart.

After so many long hours of isolated work and after so many hours of active participation in Life, we bring this book in a traditional format echoing the Primordial message to the Present and Future vocabulary for our Epoch.

We do hope these verses shall bring the pleasure of reading, conveying the message of Unity of the Mankind and much hope to all.

Fahredin Shehu

Preface

Shehu and the Literature of Solitude for the Solitude

It is of vital importance for every Nation to have its own representatives in Literary and Artistic scene of the World. Luckily Literature still remains one of the Spiritual heritage that can not be sold and merchandise as other products in the typical economic/ finance sense of meaning. It still bears some of primordial elements that transmigrate from one Culture to another thus dispersing its charm and allure the rest that seems beyond the narrow borders of respective Nation i.e. Culture.

Fahredin Shehu represents typical phenomena in the Literature sense of meaning i.e. unsold product but absorbed instead, linking the Spiritual with the Phenomenal and Manifested in the lineage of European Masters from Homer to Blake. When mentioning the lasts, *Shehu* successfully cultivates the Literature that is not for organized groups, associations, Poetry Centers but for the reader who may ponder on the most quintessential particles of LIFE. For *Shehu* the Life is the most extraordinary Phenomenon, since it is as LOVE, indescribable process, whereas DEATH is a momentum, it happens in short and fast, and there's no Magic in it.

Shehu, remains calm in the refusal from the current literary poor scene in Kosovo, since he feeds the Mind and Souls of the upcoming generation with the purely essential form of ART, which is Transcendental in a basic note, Primordial and Eternal. Having work with the Word as he transmutes it in Calligraphy and says that *The Calligraphy is the crystallization of the Creative impulse,*

Crystallization of Soul in a firm words and shapes on different medium. But what he carves in the being of reader is so much absorptive that it remains indispensable part of them. The Love he shares has the Universal values therefore it is widely accepted, translated in over 20 languages and represented in every continent. His only grotesque is his spicy humor, and after us read in one of his interviews he claimed: *"I'm published in every continent except Antarctic, thus only Penguins and Kosovars never read my Poem"*.

In his 23 years writing career produced nine published books five in Kosovo and four abroad: Macedonia, UK, Portugal, USA and many pages unpublished in traditional formats.

The last work *Shehu* produced is "Pleroma's dew", yet is another genuine work that stands between Inspiration and Revelation. The Transcendental, Noetic, Spiritual, remains simply a language that is used only in silence, and transmits what is difficult to describe where he often claims that: *"We lack Terrestrial vocabulary for the Celestial quest"*, and *"You can't learn poetry, its God's gift and it comes from His Mercy"*. It naturally depends on the taste and how much one may tolerate the truth when he sees in its Spiritual Mirror, i.e. his Soul.

The power of Individual, is strongly depicted in his work, since passing through the hell of the occupation, genocidal war, Transitional survival of the small and poor Balkan Country as Kosovo is, frankly embodies in this Literature produced by *Shehu,* where's no match in Style, Imagery, simple Artistic Language and Sincerity.

Feed by all what Men Genius created in Spiritual terms; Literature, Zen koans, Upanisadas, Sufi Masters as Rumi, Ibn Arabi and others, Cabbalists, Transcendentalists, Theosophists, Thoreau and Khalil Gibran, *Shehu*, creates uniquely with what Albanian Literature may be represented as it did in Humanity with Mother Teresa, offering to the Mankind, the hope for better World. What is vivid today in Literature trends is Plagiarism and the abyss of the surface (Baudrillard), yet *Shehu,* remains to quintessential, almost traditional elitist; difficulty to approach the real information on Self, and goes to the Kernel of the Kernel.

While much literature is written about the Illusion of the Beginning (Genesis) and of the End (Apocalypse), *Shehu* rather writes on the Illusion of the NOW and claims:

> "I'm not here to say the pride of forgotten past
> Nor do I'm here to sing miraculously
> Suras and Sutras of Holy Scriptures
> I'm here to kiss the child in the forehead;
> Where the Star has to spark its Beauty"

When he speaks about BEAUTY he says:

> "The Beauty is the Jewel
> In the Crown of Eternity and
> The hair from your skull shall bear witness"

And on Creation he wrote:

> "…with the threads of my Knowledge, Destiny and Wisdom
>
> Come in the Altar of my shrine; my heart bears Galaxies for you to pass through"

Despite all turbulences; love for the Art, Mankind, Creation and Harmony emphasized in a unique way, faces difficulties to create a special shelf in The World Literature today, since this kind of art shall in the future mark the beginning of the Theurgy in Literature, a typical realization of what Nikolai Berdyaev expected: **The world has not yet seen a religious epoch of creativeness.**
It shall indeed see in the work of Fahredin Shehu.

Visar Korenica
Septemer the 19th, 2012
Prishtna
Kosovo

Table of Contents

Dedication	v
Acknowledgement	vi
a few words from the Author	viii
Preface	ix
Being : Prelude to the Scrolls	xiv

Poetry

I ~ The Scroll Of Power	1
II ~ The Scroll Of Plethora	23
III ~ The Scroll Of Containment	63
IV ~ The Scroll Of Essence	69

Epilogue — 81

Postface	83
Fahredin's Biography	85
Fahredin's Bibliography	86
Publishings	88
Participations	93
The Gallery	97

Being : Prelude to the Scrolls

On a day when the pollen of yellow Crocus
lifted up in the air, in lined in sonorous harmony
of the vast beyond all bygones interfering adultery
remained concrete and visible past

It is the one that bore nothing more as it seems
then a goblet full of tears

He is called Chosen as the lack of determination
left him empty hands by the wine arbor in the Sun

he found his secret in the light, where even darkness
can't unveil it- The Moon was full and the upcoming
day shall be light; imperative of time so to say has
allure and parlor- Its turn to speak follows
the arrangement of known and unknown agendas

It sounds thus: I unfurl the Scrolls I bear in my heart and
keep two in the left hand and another two in the right one

for they shall reveal through "The calm eye of the storm "
an audible order what Reality has to correspond and
the laws of its correspondence shall manifest
"Different orders of reality"

What it shall reveal plus words and images
sounds and vibrations which man bore throughout eons
and named them sacerdotal

I hear it speak: nobody is forbidding you
to be good and it happen to hinder
find hindrance and kill with the smile
thus you communicate glory with gold
and the naked body of the Truth with the ivory

It advises with the ardor: you can't
forget the wrong-doing done to you
what you should" what you must as
the spiritual modes demand and they are
Fear, Love and Knowledge

You can also remember good-doing done
To you; what you must

Try to forget the wrong- doing and
remember the part of it only as lesson

Try also to remember the wholeness
of good-doing so you give lesson to others

You get married then love thy children

to multiply the volume of the circle
who envelopes you with unlimited love

Since you used to be loved by your parents and
you hardly live without love of others; therefore
you merge the chain of love for your sake

You read in order to see your surrounding soul-mate
and feel your sociability
You also read to remove the dark curtain of ignorance
but when you wish to enlighten; you follow the footsteps
of those who walked before

When you see the signs- you name them
while the traveler laugh upon since you name them
With your vocabulary and think that you have
Discovered a dimension nobody dared
To step in or go beyond

While in coenobium of yourselves you give
eloquent sermons an Ego stands and rebel;
my entire life was a struggle to become nothing
more than a normal Human
other in a hush speaks volumes of past lives
the other of the other yet silent repents
for a collective sin- the Grand ego advertises

the uniqueness of Wisdom he was gifted and
celebrates with laudable fanfare that says:
finally I realized in order to please everybody and
make them happy- you ought to forget yourself and
your entire happiness in there
you gain a spiritual liberation

Then you shall see the lips of heaven
full of blood and shinning epithelium
where there's no scarlet to compare
these lips kissed my Plexus and fertilized my womb

the Mother I shall become to eternal progeny
forever young; the embodiment of the first newborn

Shall I bestow a king to the world a wise and just?
loved by the crowd and Turba and beloved of Almighty

You may watch but touching will cost you a treasure
forbidden kingdom; the wish become a permanent
suffer of the gluttonous child is it age or is it a human
yet immature to grasp unease struggle it comes in jet;
un-intercessor for days and all what time has to offer
while I by- stand the flying fishes and the floating elephants
all over is it survival what I offer to you
who may even touch without paying a dime

FAHREDIN SHEHU

MAELSTROM

the Four Scrolls of an Illyrian Sage

A Poem by

FAHREDIN SHEHU

2012
Prishtina
Kosovo

inner child press, ltd.

I

THE SCROLL OF POWER

Being folded with The Scroll of Essence, Scroll of Plethora and the Scroll of Containment

The Scroll Of Power

On the Divine Light- for it created by all

potency what we now call the old aged

bliss that is fresh- no one can measure by any tool

all colors aim to once in a lifetime unify and

become light and all shapes dream of the cosmic mold

to become a gravity's one spot

as it all begin until it combusts and bangs

there is a Power in thy word o awakened

the infrasound is heard. It leaked through

the river of Temporality following the footsteps

of all those who float as dry willow leafs

where the Sun enjoys His beauty and magnanimity

of his potency- The water skin sparks the rays and

declares its momentum- There is indeed a huge river

taking in his journey to transport them to the Ocean

of Supra-temporality; where even a Linden flower

fragrance

The Scroll Of Power

evaporates zealously since it aims to fill the chest of

the asthmatics and dispel all earthly dirt- And when

you hear saying: "It is the way of creation aiming the final

touch and stands to become a sacred anonymous- Then

your Art is for real- then you become one- then

the existence is as it is predestined- then your

Art is for real- then your Art is objective.

Until you sip and stir your being with the vast beyond

and your name unifies with the cells of the unknown- don't expect

neither the real perception nor the essence of the color since

the essence of the color is light- it was not in vain said:

"…Let there be light! "- For the one who see is not

the same with the one who sees not

The breath that speaks - it has presented and

explained

what his treasures hides but what the incoming ray brought

to our retina- is what we shall now describe. It is a matter

in all forms and levels of manifestations, in all degrees

from invisible to a rude form- from rude to exalted

and from exalted to the sublime- We started to name

It's a Man. And the Man developed in several appearances

and climbed in various degrees- It seems he utilized

the dowry of consciousness in the best mode

He differs even from us- as he speaks… his words are

of water to ease the burning wound- where the light

of Cosmos deeply penetrates- as he utters a word of flame

He burns harshly ashes all what stands in the front

and turns to dust- As he says the word of repentance

He becomes more exalted then us and his prayer

is accepted by the Lord- We conclude: he has a Word.

Exactly…Potent!!!

The Scroll Of Power

The Man has a Pen- He writes and records

His achievements- so the Turba may follow and

Go forth- evolve. He has a pen to write on Grand

Mysteries-

Unveiled Theophanies thus conveying to the crowd

the journey of his soul- We conclude: He has a Pen.

The Man has a Will- he does what we are unable to

perform

from one extreme to another- He may remain, although

Human

-Inhuman or rather a mere protozoa yet he may exalt

beyond

the Gabriel's level and step bare-naked in the front

of the Grand Throne- He may build the brothels to sell

the human flesh of all colors and he may build a Holy

Throne of Wisdom having Hobbits, Hnomes, Spirits,

Angels,

Daemons and Salamanders as servants – As he may walk

through the gates of Hell and show his perseverance

The Gates of Paradise awaits to hear the sound of his knocking

We conclude: He has a Will.

The Man has a Thought- when he thinks he may block

the dimensions and penetrate deep in the kernel of the Universe

He has shown to us that the heart of the Sun is a freezing ice and its cover is a burning flame

He may think abundantly and remember all details and segments of the wholeness, yet he may fully stop every thought

and experience Nirvana and even step beyond Fana[1]

when he thinks- he may discover planet calculating

on his notebook while eating breakfast and

in toilet cleaning nostrils declaring a discovery of Poetry

---

[1] Sufi concept for the ultimate unification with the Divine

The Scroll Of Power

yet he's often ruled by a petty ruler of the awareness-

his Ego. We conclude: He has a Thought.

Thus discovering four main powers of Man

We shall now speak what was before him, in order to

praise the Majesty of the Almighty.

The Man has a Plot- when he release his soil and

liberates his being- when purifies his backspin

from all oceanic microorganisms and the fluid

that holds the pulp of the cord to the top crown

of the brain, is clear and tastes as sea water - it contain

as it is able to contain the attributes of Almighty

He is Compassionate, Rich, Giver, Strong and Powerful

Just and Decisive, Strong-will and full of Self-initiative

He's able to speak and the flame came out of the bush and

both in the flame that is unable to give harm

He is able to suffer for all and speak to us albeit

an illiterate shepherd made miracles. He may invent

tools that help others to elevate and fly and he

may invent stories to educate the upcoming prodigy

We conclude: He is a Container!!!

As he may contain the kernel of the Universe

in a tiny essences harmoniously beloved and

irresistible from the external irritations- He may

contain Love- the most mysterious being ever existed

and dwell in it- until they become One-existence and

rejoice the Living.

We offer you this Scroll for We understand your ability

to see the difference- It is obvious that we speak out

of love and for love- As we do it not as we utter it-

hence this has a power to embrace the petty ignorant

and illuminate – for the Love is Knowledge

of another sort and it is a power of another capability-

It becomes a Quest for established thought patterns

therefore it ought to solve with illuminated

The Scroll Of Power

mental strengths- What may seem complicated it is

out of missing vocabulary and inability

to narrate the secrets of the light- for the light

is a pure essence and it hides mystery. It blinds

the eye of terrestrial and burns the retina

of the celestial vision- when this gate is open-

You shall see everything that was hidden for eons

in all directions- what is in a front of you- you shall

see dark stones partially covered with kelp and

the trees with the spongy mushrooms embraced

by weird but gentle lianas- the sound came beneath your

feet

is our of dried broken wings and brown oak leafs and

the sound of your rhythmic breath in countdown

mixes with the smell of decayed vegetative remnants

while their Souls circulate around you as the Meccan

pilgrims

around Kabba- you are confused by your aim of arrival to a

place

people rarely succeed to step in. The silence of your vision

is a testimony of existence- Your plane is on the core?

Whatever surrounds you shall bring benefits only

if you know how to attract their benevolent nature

You shall see the Self- it is a danger void

being careless toward it you risk the age-old experiences

pass unseen- hence the world is here to show

her Beauty- not silently to chop her flesh mercilessly

and the blood of her veins is our Souls filling every…

and the most distant parts of the Grand Body.

You'll see and face the Time when the sweet- makers

speak on the Spirit evocations and the poor and mere

journalists speak about Astrology. Even babies just

ejected from the womb- shall laugh upon and not cry

instead and the holes in the Sun's surface will remain black

with the static shape- Myriads of them who can't believe in

"Now"

but remembering the suffers of the past days and

The Scroll Of Power

think over hope of the day to come are unaware

for the passing of the Now- A felt needle- leaf from

the Beirut's cedar awaits your service

it is your ear that hears and the heart that trembles

It is so when you feel emptiness from the death

of the butterfly in Kyoto and the weight felt on the skin

of the sprinkled spittle of Lama in Peru- shall seal your

indifference once you understand that the leaf from

the heaven's tree that bears your name is about to fall

in the hand of the death's Angel- It'll be late to change your

course- We know how. You created a sonorous harmony

- chanting prayers in the lamb-wool as it is a container

Of the Soul and a subtle carpets has been woven- the one

who has ever listened the sound from the carpet in the

language

unknown to her possesses ESP but the words she utters

she never understood. The thread of Wisdom is

an old cord that binds all seven bridges to the Unknown

the remaining one serves as the last for your eon for

rare are those among you who posses the ears of

understanding

it is "Us" here to show you out of Love that

the World has now to see the real maturation

of the Spiritual Maturity- It shall now seize the opportunity

as the limits of Mind's capabilities are approaching

the limits of the heart's aptitudes and the Harmony is

Now possible more than ever We stand

here, beside, up, down, in the front and behind

to facilitate and mild the foreign aggressors

of the Harmonious Pace

We are here too- as we know you went through

Gates of Hell now the Paradise waits to hear

the sound of your knocking

When you speak do not care the cantankerous

as they ought to name your parlor as: Turba Poetica

yet you know your lips of Wisdom shan't say:

The Scroll Of Power

POURUOI TOUS CES HAINE[2]

since thy word is a word of power and it

emerges from the Source of the Heart

it is the Abode of the valor and the highest secret

the throne of Kingdom below visible dimensions

which are nine not for a trillionth of millimeter

What the Abode hides- you may say nothing that

wouldn't

be presence- and the Presence is the consciousness

of the almighty that overwhelms "The All"

there's no separation and "In Presence" you are One-

existence Unified with the source- you attain nothing with

brain

You use throughout Millennia for what we shall parliament

in the Scroll is yet to be revealed- for we speak to you

in Language you best understand- hence you shall too

speak

---

[2] French -Why all these hatred?

from the altar of your Abode in a language the multitude

best understand- for you now know enough- What is certain

Knowledge and the Essence of Certitude- for you know what you

see and you see what you know; you know the Truth of Certainty

for you enter the knowledge fully immaculate and you

Saw a slop of sunrays on your naked face first, then

in your entire bare naked body- Now you know

The Truth of Certainty- Since you experience the harshness

of Ultraviolet- There's a DMM- a Dynamic Molecular Motion

in what to others seems as Harmonious Chaos, but them

produce the harmonious twists of Joy and fear but

they produce Sympathy with Contrapuntal decorated

as a dark sky with the sparkling stars and the stardust of

cadenzas falling on a gentle skin of a newborn

The Scroll Of Power

The Open-eye shall excuse us- we speak using threads of

Knowledge

Wisdom and Destiny- we speak out of Love in a Language

the Multitude understands best and it understands best

what the heart bore and shall borne for nothing is created

without Love and there's no such a long hatred that

may hinder the Sun of Love to appear on Nadir and

Horizon

Once a Man sat in the grape grains and spoke to

the grape's golden seeds- he after their discourse

extracted a secret of the seed that told the Certitude of

Certainty

and it is a cure for prostatitis many Men suffer from. But

before that

the seeds assembled and laughed upon Men criticizing

His blindness and Soul vague- just as a Poet of the world

for the eyes of the World – He in fact is the Lover and the

Beloved

He laughed upon a translator who said to a fellow- I do not understand

a word although I translated that Poem- even the speech is not

of terrestrial source- but the so- called poet in fact the Theurgist

compassionated and not laughed instead- he said: The one who faint in Love is unaccustomed to love not and

the one who wrote after this bewilderment is a Meta- Poet

so you understand not the word he utters- you ought to

experience it- as the Truth of Certainty- as the sun pampers

your naked Soul and the candle ignite your focus for the world

beyond the Gates of Darkness- Then you are able to gain from

those words the world call them Poetry and the translator

got lost on his way and in his have a soul- The so called Poem

which was the Sun's Lament for the loss of potency; was

The Scroll Of Power

published by the circle of Neo-Hyperborean residing in
the land where Marcillio Ficino exposed few secrets we
unveiled in our Tavern while gambling with the stars
all other powers but Love shall perish

Now let us please reveal few words on the letters of the
heart
Which are the keys to open the Gates of the Grand Temple
located at the most distant valleys Men have ever
encroached

If somebody ever talked to you on tears and
it didn't correspond to your knowledge and experience
Say: the tears have a spring deep in heart; they are
before every word, powerful as existence, opposite but
interchangeable with laugh- Either after sorrow
or after happiness, the enlightened sees only the difference
in nuance and transparence, despite to ordinary seems just
a liquid that is the lack of every word

when we told Plato; God created two eyes and two ears

and only one tongue- it means Men has to listen twice and

more,

to see twice and more but speak once and less- even less

so the tear shall roll to wash your being and expose

a time-self with all colors and nuances to the level

of unification and becoming light of the starry visible sky

and

of the most distant recesses of the Universe

We shall not repeat the orisons of the wise ascended from

the heaven and the wisdom descended to the Earth

for many in the past claimed prophets and in your present

there is a plenitude of false prophets, but their hearts

well know as we do… how much delusion they create

throughout turmoil of spatiotemporal secrets

semi- exposed whereas they are only more tiny mustards

in the vastness of grand Metatron and Arghal –

The all-knowing knower

The Scroll Of Power

The weak-spoiled-hearts shall circle around not knowing

how much them being ignorant and un-enlightened souls

have been suppressed- we shall now send a dove of secret

to thy heart, only an encrypted and later deciphered

message

so to give you a hint- for verily they just want to deceive

you

claiming that God Almighty put the unknown name Baduh

on the

Ring of Adam- but to which Adam we utterly ask

While you calmly observe and unable are to do anything

for rescuing the nearly exterminated Mandeans in Iraq

does anybody care if your heart mourns while?

the terror of extremists is a real plague - Many strange

things

shall occur if you live the age of your recently deceased

father

open your eyes and beware of evil. The comet shall pass

and the Venus get closer- the pressure of the Sun and

the humid air shall blacken your lungs – these are only

a signs for the turmoil, Men created on earth shan't pass

-Unpunished

There will be days when out of control you'll be in

sleepless

nights and heavy days you'll not count any longer

the moment when you'll receive the signs if you are

awaken for the Celestial quest- for the worldly things shall

trigger you not for your sake but for your most beloved

out of seeds of weeping willow the huge tree from your

heart shall

invite the subtleties of the cosmic correspondences in your

exhausted body - your bones shall echo as Canyon and

the wind shall blow and shake the leaves of your Soul

thunders from the heavy dark clouds felt upon

even the Iris wouldn't be potent enough to protect you

regardless she is of Jupiter- grand planer is your protector

The Scroll Of Power

You shall have many wants and don'ts but demands of others shall prevail so you'll forget yourself- for the faculty of your heart is Nobility- this is a testimony of your nearly prophetic message- so be it!!!

…and thus be satisfied - not hasten the decision of the Lord- for

the time is need for honey to become a blood, Rumi said to be pumped in jets and bestow the mightiest Power pf the Universe- for it is LOVE spoken, sung and done by many- periodically…

II

THE SCROLL OF PLETHORA

Being folded with the Graphene Organza of the Visible, Semi-Visible and Invisible

The Scroll Of Plethora

It is said by your sages what we have revealed to the most

lucid brains of terrestrial intellect that the time shall

come when Science shall observe old and the oldest of

Philosophy

translate all- one by one concept, after meticulous

measurement

and reckon, and when they shall approach the mystery

of Simplicity they might travel the planets and build up a

climate

weaponry- they shall too, heal few hard diseases but what

We have

revealed in the Scroll of Power they shall hardly dwell in

the abyss

of the top most layer of it- for what heart bears are a step

downward Navel, that returns Human to the source of

existence

avoiding madness Men shall search, go down to the navel

and

The Scroll Of Plethora

perhaps to the feet for abundance of knowledge in 700 000 000 nerves

of thy little head is streamline to the madness

the time shall come when imploring mysteries of the Scroll of Power

to the Scroll of Plethora shall be an urge to survive

for survival means the continuation of the will power and

the transformation through it- a real Metamorphosis

is still to come - What it was time ago called Alchemy-

now the Science

shall marry two Scrolls we descend from the Grand Father

the most luminous Intellect in Creation

a well-spring of All-Knowing Creator- it shall all be a reflection

from what is here a spatiotemporal synthesis of Love

above and below Love and a Knowing below and above

knowing, encompassing "All" in all directions.

The real change is near and soon you shall see an upgrade Alchemy when the Terrestrial shall see obviously the Celestial and

properly

utilize both forces for the influence of wide range while it

still

Remains Neutral

We have prepared you listen carefully- from the star mists

we tailored sparkling tunics and the thick books of signs

from the pages of the Universe- between the breasts of

the Mother Earth we stood to hear the sound of heartbeat

when we direct our vision toward the blue sky and see

the white clouds they change shapes and become

steamy lumps of holly Water and the sky turns scarlet

being ashamed for woman who claim to be a Poetess

but she's everlasting psychopath- yet the sky and us are

aghast with others- these "others" know the lunacy

by its grandeur but still trust to a Commingle since

it corrupts with the hidden element.

The Scroll Of Plethora

Alas!!! And thus for ages we know nothing but as you call it Poetry

for the Poem is still a visible Kinvad[3] of your rude materialism

We know People, Demons, Angel, Plant, Mineral but we never

learned how to kill- we never learned how to suck blood

of the innocent- we never learned how to bind our Souls

to gold nor did we learned… ever, how purchase a Paradise

We learned how to rejoice and embrace what Men has created

We learned too how to dance in cosmic tune and feel flutter

of the Butterfly in Mongolia- we collected the Cedar's needle- leafs

from Lebanon and read poetry on our way back from the Silk Road

and we danced with the Sufis in Konya and collected

---

[3] In Zoroastrian Religion, the remained bridge out of seven bridges that connect the Soul to the other Realms

dews from the Irish fresh green trefoil- We fed empty stomach

in Africa and empty hearts in the Balkans- We warmed cold

by ice hearts in Scandinavia and joined the prayer flags in Tibet

We offered a sacrifice to Venus in Central America's Pyramids

and collected black- pearly caviar in Iran- we drunk Lhasi in India

and being fed by Kali; the Holly Mother- We gave soul to the atheists

in Soviet Union and compassion to the greedy capitalists in the West

We read Zohar with enlightened Cabbalist Rabbis and Birhatiyah

with Muslim Ruhaniyah Masters- We made scrolls of Upanisadas and broke the Roman Cross- we perfumed Jesus with Jasmine essence

and fed Bodhisattva with nettle leafs to rescue him from the starvation

We said openly to the politicians: Spare us from your lies

otherwise we'll ascend to heavens for another cycle

of 80 000 years as Enoch- although they don't care at all

Here ends our Sublime word- then under the shade of huge old nut tree

seat carefully for piece of the moment and peal the green full of Iodine shell

to see the miraculous kernel. This is fruit and seed in the same time

it is the brain of all plants and it helps your brain too.

As the Miracles of thy Lord are spread so as we said to Plato- "you have

two eyes to see twice and more to ponder on the heavenly dowry which compared to the wealth in flocks in here are just a mustard seed

beware of nut tree as it attracts thunder which even Iris can't save you

It is all here…passing through the Labyrinth of cerebral canyons

to zealously accomplish resolutions of all enigmas- walking and

whirl-pooling in an Audible void until hears seven different voices

where the Aquatic Abyss waits to host furiously - It is all here…

the starry sky of brain- since indeed… there exists everything what Mind

can imagine, even what Mind cannot imagine- it exists for Existence

is Absolute- composed of relative existing fragments- You may call this

The Scroll Of Plethora

a stellar parlor from the Cerebral Constellations- even- Exasperatingly

obvious Truth but walking on the winds and above waves of lust

passing through the Loom of Deceitfulness thither exist and a greasy

pitch of sins- Unconsciousness of your Celestial origin- May indeed

transform you into a vermin then you shall see what the rabbit hides.

Today let the drop of Celestial dew glittering on the petal of your heart

fall early when the world is still asleep and covered with the dreamy

mattress- let it to precipitate in the bottom where the pearl shall

sparkling the entire body- you live in the Kingdom of Ignorance and this pearly-radiance shall at least bring some light- but stay until

there would be your seed of Liberty then you shall see the Gate to

the Corridor of Salvation- This leads to the Gate of Kingdom of Knowledge

that has the prison of the Self- in self you shall find the gate that leads

to the Kingdom of Wisdom- the tunnel that leads to the Scroll of Power

We know so far of you- we are proud off- you have exquisite disability

to Hate- so we let you speak even when you are pissed off- so we record

Your speech:

I'm pissed off people eloquent in speech- empty in hearts

The Scroll Of Plethora

I'm pissed off Scholars full of knowledge- empty of Knowing and

pissed off all who love with the tongue instead of heart- the Aquatic void

of their delusion- I'm pissed off too of people who claim creativity but

never destroyed their handcraft- I'm pissed off all who piss in the pot

and never see themselves mirrored beneath the hot foam of their urine

I'm pissed off of people with hate alert- does it

meticulously just because I'm Black?

Poor, all religious and none of them crippled and disabled to hate

I'm pissed off people who lie and lazy are for the cord of lie is too

antique and it is luscious by obvious to my eyes and the lazy who does nothing but builds the Tower of cells to be dismantled by worms

and vermin in and out of Sepulcher- I'm too pissed off…

all those who declared knowledge disowning it since Socrates

appears to me as a last child on Planet; a Geo-Spiritual Child

I'm also pissed off …all who eavesdrops the mysteries of the starry sky

to murmur them in the ears of ignorance for Ignorance has pilled blankets

of layered knowledge but naked *en gross* of Knowing- Life is the most

extraordinary as it lasts- Death is a moment of power yet never overcomes

itself- for the Life overcomes everything even own-self"- We exclaim: "Bravissimo"

The Scroll Of Plethora

You have learned a subtle difference between Man and

man, between Soul and Spirit

between Heart and Myocardium between Brain and

Cerebrum and it is all here-your

passage to the shores of Midnights and abundant forests of

your evergreen

vegetative Soul- We know there in your dwelling Men shall

laugh upon you

and compete who shall faster and more harshly pile the

labels and the labels shall

sound- bad language borrowed and spirit lack of harmony

with attempt to create

a personal paradise- a lunatic with eccentric behavior self

appraising poet

but stay calm as you aren't a Poet since the Poets are

eccentrics and

You are not, since the Poets lie and you don't…you may

crow as rooster

early in the morning while they are asleep since you saw

the Angel

but avoid and please run in midday when the asses among

them

start braying say the word LOVE as it saves you from their

braying.

Indeed you ought to be happy today as you frequently hear

crowing

of the rooster- there's a flock of Angels and their Sovereign

to lead you

ahead and make shade of Light- while you read the signs

and letters of

the Universe- creating beautiful stanzas eloquent and lucid

in you liberty and freedom the dark wings of the bat had

had gone

for farthest then the black night may blur the beauty of the

dusk

here we stand for you… oh Thought of Royalty… oh exalted Father

with the overwhelming embrace of Intelligence- truly Men has gone

far reaching the highest peak- for Maturity means Freedom and Potency

as a wind pool rotating, taking away particles, segments, limbs and depicted

beautifully the Beauty which is the giant ruby in the Crown of Eternity

as we go on- You ought not to reduce the space of your being- since we

have yet to unfurl the Scroll of Essence- there you may see the Glamour

and Nobility but still to come…

We shall also here say to you a few explanatory words to ponder upon and it is about this Maelstrom older than Atlantis and these Four Scrolls

they unfurl to you- they have their kinship with the Farsi Ilm-e- Kshnoom[4]

Indian Gita[5], Muslim and Hebrew Scriptures- you hear us saying:

the buds of restrain have opened ardently- we gaze the blueprints

of the curious Eyes on its delicate skin and the desire we left behind long ago

in a sad orphanage, now they mourn for the path we are in; and surely wouldn't

lead us astray- give us only a slip of sunray if you will so?

all shall see through the lens of the Good-Will; the All; we offer

zealously; and we also speak about Wild Wisdom and you hear us say:

---

[4] Farsi/ The Book of Zoroastrian Occult Knowledge
[5] Bhagvad Gita- one of the most beautifully sacral Book of Indian Heritage referring to Lord Krsna

elements and elementals and the weight of Eons good and evil, smell and

skunk and the burden of time- you who spoiled my purity mere senile secluded in the deep forests hiding your misery cowards fearing Life's defeats and refusals- scared of Love for life and all what brings forth the Paradise as we wish so to say

and, and, and, and, and, and… who cares for the moral of this tuned

something beyond Heaven and Hell who revoke Earth unveiling

unfortunately, the obvious truth in your most diluted blindness

alas, alas, alas, alas, alas, alas, alas, alas, alas and Alas!!!
We bede Knowledge that is gloomy and the yesterdays Wisdom

which is today's nonsense- the giant dormant- awakes with the touch of creativity and tuned with the Universe- for it was fed by the milk of the Truth which is the Conscience of the Life

as the apricot releases its magic smell as unique as Life- we say

the apricot, is apricot, is apricot, is apricot…a celestial grammar

of a childish desire to remain a recall of the unique smell beyond

comparison by none- by appearance, by being if you wish so

by existence…by existence…by existence…by existence and

there you find the pleasure when the pleasure exceeds the high

of a standing Man with the raised hand- know that life has

given you the moment above your possibility to realize that

and the mind within-beneath your precious self stands firm as

a cord- ray of the Sun as a firm pillar of Knowledge in the basement of course fairness, justice, liberty and the spa of wisdom

surround all

there is a bridge; a narrow gateway both way possible;

lucky is the one who goes back from one hemisphere of

brain

to another and finds a perfect balance- rare is the one

who knows Algebra and Grammar in the same

time…Equally

for having a compass of behavior in "Now", is a blissful

accomplishment- lucky is the one among Men who posses

serenity in a chaotic overwhelmed communication of what

is percept, what is heard, what is felt- and all of these

simultaneously

without losing a dime of Wealth- now you shall realize that

the Soul

has no weight and matures slower than any of your limbs

you post yourself in a distance between two steps of a little

girl

your left hand catches the elbow of the right one punching the wall

of clay; what is pure and clear as sound of falling crystal on

an icy stone plate echoes deeply in a serene heart- you who opened

the ears of understanding- verily your hearts have a vast space

for everything beautiful- The Men is beautiful, The Animal is beautiful,

the Plant is beautiful, the Mineral is beautiful, the Air is beautiful

for verily the one who sees Beauty and delivers the good sounds to all

the Universe awards in myriads- for the merits of the good-doing

attaches to you tightly to the very existence of the Universe and

this is not a mere thing- for the one who possesses reason

detach yourself once again from the basics of the lust and you

shall see how the Sun shines from within- Abandon your temporal

desires but live in Mentation of the crowd and you shall

understand that you are not an Eremite for ascetism seems to us

an affirmation and confession of weakness and cowardness

Live with Life and through it and you shall see that all Holy Scriptures

are sealed in the stones and their letters and sentences are widely-

open exposed in the leafs of all trees, in the sounds of river, in the voices

of all birds- the beautiful singers, in all shine of precious stones and the inner warmness of the coal, in the sacrifice of the Pelican and in

the cry of a child

let your mind pulses freely- it is a reservoir of will-power

train your brain and make it stronger as muscles then you

shall see

the mental faculties in their youthful eruption and potency-

then you

may see your mirror keeping forever your image as a

Dynamic Painting

in a wooden frame with the golden glazure- you shall also

see the seals

of her gazing and wild glance in your skin afterwards, to

keep them

in a velvet box of wedding earrings of your Mother, the

collected

glances as dots of curiosity.

There is a tree in Japan waiting for you, with the leafs of

dichotomy

The Scroll Of Plethora

waiting you from the ice age. They call it Gynkyo that survived

the worst human devastating power. It survived the blast in Hiroshima and Nagasaki. Have we spoken to you about the Fig?

Don't we? - for that plant is the most evolved among all plants

and its secret is hidden in the fruit which is flower and the fruit

in the same time- we have indeed talked to you about Olive and her holiness and Aloe and her powers.

Next to a quagmire a flying hippocampus moves

in velocity with the tiny wings that enlivens the hearts

of the Alive- by every move something good happens in another

Galaxy- Call him and he shall respond- scarifying him for

your health; Tie on your right shin with the red silk thread and you shall see the healing wonders.

We have also spoke to you on Rumi and the secret of weeping reed

but more on this we expose details in the Scroll of Essence

We sent a wise king to your Knowledgeable and Acknowledgeable.

He got very blue eyes more blue than Azure Sea.

He knew over 400 plants for many diseases.

He produced beer from honey and barley and was just and made

the Kingdom prosper- now rare is a just King among Men because

formerly Politics was Art, now became Science. Verily we have

nothing against Science but it is yet an infant religion you can't

transcend in the next thousand Men years.

The Scroll Of Plethora

Once the Time was a Goddess to you until you started to measure it

but who can measure something immeasurable- She always lived

in a vast ruby valley but her aging powers are stronger than that

of Sun and all Galaxies- She stretches them in all directions touching

every one known semi-known and unknown- She is more powerful

than every joint brain and She subordinates only to the Absolute

She shall offer a space to you when you'll achieve the speed

of light- She then may embrace you in her Abode and marry

You Enlightened Soul- see now you're aging and Drink Rum on

a Shore: Everything is becoming mysterious:

The feathers of the raven and the gems from the depths

of the earth; Men and Women alike wandering - What is

holy

and what profane repertoire of outrageous sounds

The sea-foam bringing corpse of sometime Creatures full of

life-

Red corrals and spawns of whales with the smell of

Ocean's basement.

The elders on the shore sitting- having small glasses of

Rum

rolling the dice; who shall better host the Death; while She

awaits for the bed where to nap for a while; undressing her

aquamarine brocade and heavy accessories from

the metals of the seven mountains of the heart

…and the odor She releases allures even the most agnostics

and disbelievers: She is calm and tranquil as potent as

Queen but

The Scroll Of Plethora

She dares not to knock on the door of the orphan.

I see…She has compassion for me or perhaps She isn't ordered yet

to kiss me in the forehead where the blood-spots draw

the constellation of Sagittarian.

I invoke the name of Mother and summon spirits of the distant earths

since the celebration started, when the banquet is set up by

the grand breasts Nymphs- Apsaras[6]: If there's a Paradise somewhere

it descended here so I become dead before death that happens

in a blast of a moment and in trillion's part of millimeters

where another dimension is experiencing a diffusion of a new

---

[6] Big tits Nymphs who allured Buddha

Big Bang and Supernovas- cosmic babies are Milked by

Mother.

I call in my dwelling- a serene settlement of "Us" – all of

us

who never got enough of Love, who once learned to Love

never is unaccustomed to Love not- Now listen the speech

of the

Bird King:

Heavy and deep burns- a tremendous pain

There's a Soul aches too; it torments far beyond expected

The grandeur of it is indescribable. No parlor may resurrect

the body

of Suffer. There's no twice burned by Love ashes of the

first time

remains. Seals of wisdom the bezels of which are blinding

the All

the axis of which is whirling around itself till it collapses.

The Scroll Of Plethora

When the reason lapse the mortals laugh upon

the pathway then leads to the unnamed streets- not a single mark

shows the direction to death – the envoys of which are hardly

waiting to embrace?

The hug becomes suffocation.

The kiss becomes the one of the Dragon.

The smile becomes a nasty child.

The tears become sharp- edged crystals.

The blood becomes pomegranate ruby granules.

The lymph becomes Billaminate thread.

The spawn becomes nacre.

The breath becomes a cord to heaven.

The voice becomes chopping flesh Echo.

The vision becomes a heavy mist.

The move becomes as solid monument.

The corpse becomes as poor as desert.

The memory of the Spirit only continues to narrate-

perhaps

nostalgically recall the past lives and mourns the lack of

opportunity

to repeat the same sin. Its laments are recorded in the

Scrolls

of heaven as missed chances of repetitive bigotry not as

burning desire

to diminish fear and discover the unknown.

Oh Poet…it is all you to blame… if you can not say what is

true

and what is certitude- who can?

If you do not outcry for the misbehave of dummies and

denounce the harsh aggressors- who can?

If you don't overthrow the perverse kings

and Nobles- who can?

The Scroll Of Plethora

If when a sting of wasps penetrates

the skin of the child and you don't revolt-

- Who will?

When the sluts are burning in everlasting fire

and you don't extinguish- who will?

When the drunker wanders from tavern

to another and you don't show the path-

- Who shall?

When the witches cast spells and hexes and

summon Jinns and gnomes- you don't punch with

Malleo Dei[7] - who will?

When the greedy bankers and bloody neo- imperialists

exploit the mass- you don't remove the delusion-

- Who will?

---

[7] The Hammer of God

When the Lie of the artist and goldsmith

markets justice and you don't break

the backspin of the Lie - who shall…?

When the rebel leader draw the nation together

and you don't join- who shall?

When the oracles foretell the upcoming riot and

you don't warn- who shall?

When the nymphs and fairies play the lyre

and seduce disoriented youth on the river bank

and you don't sing- who shall?

May your writing hand be crippled?

If you don't write on Love

and your eyes becomes blind if you

don't see Love.

The Scroll Of Plethora

May your tongue be knotted in nine knots

if you don't show the Truth of Certitude and

may your Soul be forever cursed if you cease

Loving- for the Love is the attribute of the Beloved

and the Spirit of the Bird King

After the bird King spoke ardently "The Integralist"

had his last Parliament to the Nacre Soul Creative:

Am I still a certain someone who walks bare naked feet?

on the prickly thorn path of searching for the Beauty

…and she remains the jewel in the crown of eternity with

the scarlet lips kissing the Divine.

While the mortals market their ignorance throwing daggers

of stupidity to hush the audience that bewilder with the

colors

of the poison dispersed unjustly for the public did not

deserve

Such a contamination

blood spilling hatred radiating in the air to dismiss the luminous

body of the seeker- who utters only the words of heart.

which the concubines couldn't spoil- neither the rich Father with

unlimited mercy- He is called: The "Integralist"

Yet we ought to write the Manifesto for the Art he brought from

the highest heavens down to obey the thirsts of the impure

mouths of the cantankerous shan't remain hidden!

As the Narrator… by stand- his efforts and see what lay in

the hearts of Men, He wants to Unite because Galaxies

have had assembled and the Universe opened His chest and

the mercy

unfolds the subtle Muslin to dress the naked Truth.

The Scroll Of Plethora

He calls upon reason- The Grand reason

and the Art- The grand Art: He calls then the Heart- the

Grand Heart

to wave the tripartite thread of Divine for He knows the

Men- still

have chance if the men compete in Good-doing

and here the Manifesto is being drafted:

Ye Man- You are created to better know each other

henceforth the hatred

shall exist only as sign- a lesson how not to behave.

Ye Man- all forms of belief are in Mind: What remains in

the Heart is Trust

so build Trust in the settlement of Soul, thus you undergo

the turbulence, fear

and jealousy and transcend the growth of phases of yours.

Ye Man- all forms of art, whether realistic or abstract,

plastic or spiritual

whether form, shape, sound, color, nuance, number and

mathematical Plethora

Noun and Grammatical Pleroma

They're all at your disposal; lucky is the one

who may integrate all for the all?

Ye Man- let the terrestrial hold the celestial

so you await the progeny that speaks a language everybody

understands-

so he speaks angelically- so the word glows as white

as neon light pure and totally unpolluted.

Ye Man- behold from the falsehood for it spoils

radioactively everything

what human Genius has succeeded to bring forth.

The Scroll Of Plethora

Ye Man- create by the force given to you From the

Universe; for Creation

is the main Attribute of vastness and fulfill- ness.

Ye Man- sacrifice for the sake of Love- ONLY for the

Love rewards

in myriad when the mind blocks and unable is

to count such a dowry.

Ye Man- bath in the Spa of the Divine and you shall see

recuperated body

The reanimated Soul for it has the drops from the most

complex Elixirs.

Ye Man- don't be afraid of my loss for the wisdom lays in-

down

to the shores of the Divine and the gate keepers are to give

you

the keys for endurance and the locks for your treasures

hidden as Sin.

Ye Man- forgive the wrong- doer as you do with the child

for he's immature and

His Soul is fuzzy with the multiple layers and he'll come to

regret or not

That doesn't make any difference.

Ye Man- sing the life for Life is a celebration never

repeated in such

a form and singing is the attribute of Existence for every

motion

gives a Sound as reward.

Ye Man-Laugh the Life, for the Laughing is the Certainty

of

the Cosmic Truth and in it there is a quintessence of

Certainty given

to the True Nature of Creation.

The Scroll Of Plethora

Ye Man- LOVE- Love all or All for Love is the attribute of the Almighty where you can find better Essence to compete with

…for it is the highest strength that destroys the most concrete walls

and undergoes all barriers.

Since it is the only power that may integrate, since integrated we

become all as we become all we remain nothing and nothing

is the name of the being and the being turn to be You.

III

THE SCROLL OF CONTAINMENT

Being folded with the Honeycomb of Light that contains Secret if the Light above Light

The Scroll Of Containment

There is a Men everyday fighting and unable is to delegate

a duty as the brain does to every organ living in harmony

for this Men has still to mature- perhaps better tame their

rude lusts- the Sun has enough rays for everybody

the Earth is huge, rich and abundant all it ever needs

is the restoration of Harmony and implementing the

Balance.

The Ocean is huge, rich and abundant; there is enough

space

and food; creatures one more beautiful than the other.

The Mountains are high and pikes of heaven are strong,

rich and abundant.

The Air in there is sparsely and healthy; it enlivens the

Earth and

her bearings- Ah those forests with heavy shade some slip

of sunray

penetrating down to pamper the beauty of tiny violets- that smell

of the decayed leafs and wigs, the lianas folding-

embracing the trunks

of huge trees and the beautiful bunches of golden bough with a sticky

mistletoe pearls decorated- that gurgle of the spring

between dark pale rocks

and the abundant water fauna in full livelihood- the mushrooms of all sorts

and colors and a healing smell of Oak moss- the chain of life is there

a living dream the crystal of which is what Men zealously chopping.

It has a core in sexuality which says: "at a long human time ago we have

revealed on sex; for the copulation is a holy act and by each ejaculation;

The Scroll Of Containment

myriads of gates of Paradise open- a fragrant petit grain essence and that

of Clary Sage and Lemon Balm and the beds for rosary for the long necks

of Angels are formed out of its radiance. Celibacy may be temporal

to pursue the Sedes Sapientiae[8]- yet for the Men it ought not to last

over forty Human days- whereas Sex is organic diaphanous pattern

of the Soul where it manifests its unconscious quintessence".

Another has been said by our Sovereign that few has been sent down

to Babylon and taught a science which human have overturned and

---

[8] The Throne of Wisdom

corrupted- then called Black, they cursed and casted spells and hexes

they call it Magic as something in comprehensible out of reach

of ordinary fellow; sowed fear and gained superiority as a childish

as every pre-potency may be- as it turns to be another malady

of Men out of control and as harmful as Men can be.

Beware o Seeker; O king of Word from such malicious

interference in knowledge that is out of reach for ignorant and

those who cannot control their instincts that demand time

to be genetically controlled; with the brutal

honesty of yours- there stands a devil and he has a blue eyes where he

craftily hides his evil- Verily…devil is not a female as your Macho

The Scroll Of Containment

projected throughout ages- just to demonize female and

gain control

over her; for the one who hates doesn't need any reason;

Sufficient enough is that you only get the Sunrays in a

winter

garden before, due and after each holiday you happily

celebrate.

IV

THE SCROLL OF ESSENCE

Being folded with all Scrolls of Wisdom, Knowledge, Craft, Art, Theurgy, Revelation

The Scroll of Essence

The Soul has no weight and matures slower than any of you limbs- When the wind blows hard and you see only its inner side; there's a force that triggers all and everything in has its own history- when the limbs are stretched

from Nadir to Horizon you see Aurora has all sorts of colors that bewilders even the most skeptic- there a child was born of a great future; the black Elk is his companion and the best friend- None of witches dare to bewitch since his guardian is Jupiter. Many have tried to steal the child who shall later become the leading force and cosmic power to restore the Peace on Earth and bring joy to the most mercilessly mistreated- The inner part of his Soul just as the inner part of the wind is very forceful and collects the rays

from the stars, quasars and has a potency of supernovas- yet

the Divine harmony within had married a Goddess-Time and space so his spatiotemporality is beyond any capture

From the hissing sound of even most advanced techno

utilities- he shall never abandon Trust as it is the only

bridge that leads to Divine nor he shall ever quit loving

for Love is the only power that transmutes the evil to Good.

He shall exercises is extremities but his Soul shall always

remain feminine- his parlor is a liquid and the harshest

Enemies become neck in his presence. Once a white Wolf

howled in his way back to Palace but the howl turned a

muslin

thread and diaphanous textures folding his strong body

to protect from other aggressors- there will be clash of

forces

of fire and water but he is the sole who shall explain that

the Water is a progeny of the Fire and there shall be Peace.

His wisdom is composed from the radiance of the stars

and the cosmic bodies and the sparks from every living

creature who keeps all those dormant but he shall be able

The Scroll of Essence

to absorb wisdom from all and respond to all needs.

His smile is a reflection of the Universe and its image
whereas upon his laugh; dimensions are created- having
a dynamic creative laugh has this faculty that only
extremely rare
have among Men… being such developed- once a Man
wanted to
approach; striving to expel his fictive Catatonia- it was a
woman
more beautiful than any fairy ever passed forth for your
vision
to be catch and kept the image of a lasting memory.

She was the one with the left marble eye and the right more
red
than any ruby. Wandering in the vortexes of all fluids until
she
got the silken thread of wind inside the grand valley.

She came by and stood forth. Nothing but despair she felt when

she revealed that Soul she thought is Male turn to be Female and

the endorsing blueprint of it was neither Male nor Female.

She left speechless for who knows how many Man Years afar.

Let us now speak to you on purity. For the essence is a real and

for real it is pure emanation- listen Son whether young lad or

senile who soak the rays of life with the earthen straw. Verily

The One has no beginning nor may the End. You have encountered

this long ago and it remains a cadaver unless repeated.

The Scroll of Essence

Don't you think that your sacred chant does not produce galaxies within chiliad part of millimeter and the star has uttered a word after being seen as light; being visible for ages more or rare has Men mentioned that

It is He with His He-ness, called by Sages: The Father who endowed
Men with the tulip of the Mind which holds a Cup; the liquid elixir of
Wisdom and made Men to sing of at first- Out of Mind He made the Mind
of Mind that bore the Sensible World and it came to Existence by shaping
energy of Mind, who now is the Architect of matter called too: The Mind
Son of Mind- thus the intelligible flame possesses the Essence of all things
for its Sparks- He made the Nature to be the Mantle of Goddess Mother and

baptized her with the *nomen barbarum* TAMARA- the little Divine Lioness.

From Her Mouth who is the Great Mother of souls; the Melody is shaping

words and says:" The Soul has a perfect measure, rhythm, balance and

perfection and it spins throbbed with the Divine. Her hair is a bristled mane

of light and her grace creates galaxies in her gracious Divine spinning dance

from the Mouth of Son who is Soul borne by the Great Mother you may hear:

"After the Father's thinking, you must know, I, the Soul, dwell, making all

Things to live by Heat"[9]

We have heard Him speak of four Worlds in the Essence for the Essence

---

[9] C 18, Chaldean Oracles by Mead

The Scroll of Essence

sleeps in this Scroll and it is now revealed to you.

The four Worlds are: the World of Emanation, the World of Creation,

The World of Formation and the World of Action.

The World of Emanation being the Divine Fire ascend to the Manifested World

The World of Creation being the Divine Water

The World of Formation being the Divine Air

The World of Action being the Divine Earth.

Similarly to your four Worlds spoken by Master Agrippa Von Nettesheim

when his Art was in its climax and they are seen as:

Divine things, Celestial things, Terrestrial things and things that will exist

in the future- Whereas in Essence they remain a mathematical model

of single digits, decade, hekatontad and chiliad for the great force

of Creation is vigorous and exceeds all even what the Tulip

of the Mind may contain and imagine- things exists beyond

imaginable

and dreamt- even imagination is unable to go that far, to

exceed

the limit of the tulip of the Mind.

In the Manifested World there is galactic coil of Soul

we've ardently twisted to create what is attracting other

cosmic

creatures to the Axis of the Divine.

The Scroll of Essence

~ FINIS ~

The Scroll of Essence

EPILOGUE

Postface

Here we end our parlor we have verbatim interpreted to you from the mighty king of the wisdom- today you count as Human. Long time ago when gods and goddesses have encroached the soil of the earth, we have spoken to a Liburnian goddess of fertility and abundance they use to call her Ansoica.

In nowadays Croatia, the Liburnians had had a splendid life. As you today bear that blood and your kernel has its genetics O mighty king of Knowledge we bestow to you these Scrolls so you give back to Mankind what you have absorbed from the Sun, constellations, Us and Sages that walked alone in a brutal honesty and possessed a Wild Wisdom, who were not arrogant nor self- appraising fellows, who lived in their poverty with the dignity different from those of Kings and Nobles, who knew the Mystery of the Letter, Number, Limbs, Heart, Soul and

Essence of Visible, Semi-Visible and Invisible things, who melted as snowflakes in an icy cold sunrays at the end of the winter; in the Essence of the Divine.

We stand firm in our awareness that rare are those who shall absorb our words, yet we know that rare are the Kings of Words and more rarely nowadays among Men you find the King of Wisdom.

So by the glimmering light of these words and a glossy sparks of the Abyss of the Surface we are concluding: WORK, KNOW, LOVE and ENLIGHTEN for these are the keys that opens the gates of the World beyond the shriek of which yearn to hear and faint then stay so for Eternity and a day more.

Fahredin

Fahredin's Biography

Born in Rahovec, South East of Kosova, in 1972. graduated at Prishtina University, Oriental Studies.

Actively works on Calligraphy discovering new mediums and techniques for this specific for of plastic art.

Certified expert in Andragogy/ Capacity Building, Training delivery, Coaching and Mentoring, Facilitating etc.

In last ten years he operated as Independent Scientific Researcher in the field of World Spiritual Heritage and Sacral Esthetics.

Fahredin's Bibliography

Published Books :

- NUN- collection of mystical poems, 1996 author's edition

- INVISIBLE PLURALITY- Poetical prose, 2000, author's edition

- NEKTARINA- Novel, Transcendental Epic, 2004, publishing House, Rozafa Prishtinë- project of Ministry of Culture Sport and Youth of Kosova

- ELEMENTAL 99- Short poetical mystical stories, 2006, Center for positive thinking, Prishinë

- KUN- collection of transcendental lyrics, 2007, Publishing House LOGOS-A, Skopje, Macedonia

- DISMANTLE OF HATE, E-book 2010, Ronin Press, London,

- CRYSTALINE ECHOES, Poetry, Hard copy and e-book 2011, Corpos Editora- Porto, Portugal

- PLEROMA'S DEW, Poem, Hard copy and Kindle/ Amazon Edition, 2012 Inner Child Press, New York, USA

- EMERALD MACADAM, Essays, Columns, Opinions, Presentations, Academic papers on Culture, Art, Spirituality, 2012, Positive Initiative, Prishtina, Kosovo

- MULBERRIES, Novel, Hard copy, LOGOS-A- Skopje, Macedonia, 2012

- HONEYCOMB, Novel, Orbis NSH-Prizren, Kosovo, 2013

- THE PEN, Arhipelag, Poems, Belgrade, Serbia 2013

Publishings : Papers and Magazines:

The Book of Poetry E-Book in Ronin press, **London, UK**

The book of Poetry in Nadwah Press, **Hong Kong**

Poetry on Magazine of Center for Humanistic studies GANI BOBI, Prishtinë, **Kosovë**

Essays on Journal "Oriental Studies", Kosova Orientalist's Association. **Kosovë**

Poetry in Magazine STAV- Tuzla, **Bosnia and Herzegovina**

Poetry in Magazine ZIVOT- Sarajevo, **Bosnia and Herzegovina**

Poetry in Magazine ULAZNICA- Zrenjanin, **Vojvodina**

Poetry in Magazine URRA- Tirana, **Albania**

Poetry in Magazine POETA- **Belgrade, Serbia**

Poetry in Magazine, ISTANBUL LITERARY REVIEW, **Istanbul, Turkey**

Poetry in Magazine, MOBIUS MAGAZINE, **New York, USA**

Poetry in Magazine OBELISK, **Tirana, Albania**

THE WORLD POETS QUARTERLY (multilingual) VOLUME No. 58, **Bei Jing, China**

THE WORLD POETS YEARBOOK 2009, **Bei Jing, China**

Poetry at Sarajevske Sveske 2010, **Sarajevo, Bosnia**

Poetry in Balkan writers, **Belgrade, Serbia**

Poetry at Poetas del Mundo, **Santiaogo de Chile**

Poetry at Mediterranean, **Gotteborg, Sweden**

Poetry at Aquillrelle, **Brussels, Belgium**

Poetry at Poem hunter, **USA**

Poetry at World Poets Society, **Athens, Greece**

Poetry at Albpoem, **Albania**

Poetry at Soylesi Poetry Magazine, **Istanbul, Turkey**

Poetry at revista ura, **Tirana, Albania**

Poetry at Uzina Marta, **Brasil**

Poetry at Arabic Nadwah, **Hong Kong**

Poetry Romanian version Orientul Meu, **Bucharest, Romania**

Poetry at Agonia , **Bucharest, Romania**

Poetry and profile at Carty's Poetry Journal, **Dublin, Ireland**

Poetry and profile at Blue Max Magazine, **Dublin, Ireland**

Poetry at Middle East Online, **London**

Poetry in English on The Sound of Poetry Review, **Argentina**

Poetry at Le post, **Paris, France**

Poetry at Aube, **Paris, France**

Poetry at 24 heures, **Geneve, Zwitzerland**

Poetry at Tribune de Geneve, **Geneve, Switzerland**

Poetry and Calligraphy at World Art Friends, **Portugal**

Poetry at lechasseurabstrait. Publisher, Patric Cintas, RAL,M Revue d'Art, et litterature, Musique, **Paris, France**

Poetry at Arte Poetica, **Salvador**

Poetry at Carcinogenic Poetry, **Brasil**

Poetry at Album Nocturno, **Salvador**

Poetry at Fernando Sabido Sanchez, **Madrid, Spain**

Poetry at Anthology Poetas Siglo Veintiuno, Editor, Fernando Sabido Sanchez, **Madrid, Spain**

Poetry at **CHECK POINT POETRY, Le Reti di Dedalus, Italy**

Poetry at **Author India, India**

Poetry at Pagina de Andres Morales, **Chile**

Poetry at Cinosargo, **Arica, Chile**

Poetry at Grey Scale, **Nigeria**

Poetry at Snow in Guinea Magazine, **13 º NUMBER OF LITERARY MAGAZINE LVII No. of 2nd etapa/01-07-2011**

Poetry at **La Granada, No. 2, Oslo, Norway**

Poetry at Othervoices.org. **USA**

Poetry at Poetry Blis Anthology, **India, 2012**

Poetry at Healnig World Anthology, **New York, USA**

Poetry at Aquillrelle, **Brussels, Belgium**

Poetry at Letras TLR, **Mexico City, Mexico**

Poetry at Realidades Y Fictiones, ed. Hector Zabala, **Buenos Aires Argentina**

Poetry at Poemish, **USA**

Poetry at Best Poems Encyclopedia, **USA**

Poetry at Froward Poetry, **UK**

Poetry at Ann Arbour Review, **Michigan, USA**

Poetry at Coldnoon Lityerary Magazine, **Jawharlal Nehru University, New Delhi, India**

Articles in www.worldbulletin.com, **Istanbul, Turkey**

Articles in www.newropeansmagazine.com, **Strasbourg, France**

Poetry Anthology for the rights of Hazara People, **Oslo, Norway, 2014**

You find Fahredins Books Here :
http://www.archive.org/search.php?query=creator%3A%22Fahredin%20Shehu%22

USA

Participations:

- Exhibition of Calligraphies in Cairo, Egypt, 2004
- Sarajevo 44th Poetry Meeting, Sarajevo 2005
- Congress on 600th anniversary of the work of Abdurrahman Ibn Khaldun, Cairo, Egypt, 2006
- Meeting for the ethnic minority rights, European Parliament, Bruxelles, 2006
- Exhibition of paintings and calligraphies at the Ministry of Culture and Tourism, Cairo Egypt, 2007
- Participation on the Congress on 800th anniversary of a Persian Poet RUMI, organized by
- UNESCO/Albania and Saadi Shirazi Foundation, Tirana, Albania, 2008

- Participation at the International conference on Islam and Balkan- Identity and building bridges, Canakkale, Turkey, 2010
- Participation at 13th International Sheikh Tousi Conference, Qom, Teheran, Mashhad, Iran, 2010
- Participation at Conference on Regional Cooperation, Kopaonik Serbia, 2011
- Participation at International Poetry Festival Voix de la Mediterranee, Lodeve France, 2011
- Participation at Struga Poetry Events- 50th anniversary, Struga Macedonia, 2011
- Participation at Nisan Poetry Festival in Maghar, Galilee, Nazareth, Israel, 2012
- Fermoy Poetry Festival in Fermoy, Ireland, 2012- confirmed but not participated due to Kosovo limitation to travel through Europe.
- Literary Workshop and Festival, Valetta, Malta, August 2013,

Translated in English, French, Italian, Spanish, Serbian, Croatian, Bosnian, Macedonian, Roma, Swedish, Hebrew, Turkish, Arabic, Romanian, Persian, Mongolian, Chinese, Maltese, Sicilian, Frisian, Polish.

Ambassador of Poets to Albania by Poetas del Mundo, Santiago de Chile

Member of World Poets Association

Member- Publishing and Editing Committee- Kosovo Ministry for Culture, Youth and Sport.

Member at the Kosovo PEN Center

Gold Medal Award and Certificate, Axlepino Publishing, Philippines, 2013

Pleroma's Dew

the Poetry of

Fahredin Shehu

THE
GALLERY

Fahredin Shehu ~ Maelstrom

Fahredin Shehu ~ Maelstrom

Fahredin Shehu ~ Maelstrom

Sus funciones son:
- Representar oficialmente en Albania al Movimiento Poetas del Mundo y mantener en funcionamiento el Cuerpo Diplomático en su país.
- Informar sobre los eventos en su país que sean de interés para los Poetas del Mundo.
- Proponer el ingreso de nuevos poetas en calidad de "Miembros" o "Cónsules en Argentina" a Poetas del Mundo.
- Ofrecer la fuerza de su palabra y ponerla al servicio de la humanidad.
- Apoyar el esfuerzo poético de los poetas del mundo en su misión diplomática por la PAZ en el mundo, la JUSTICIA (única para todos), la IGUALDAD (efectiva entre todos los habitantes de la tierra), la LIBERTAD (la verdadera, no la artificial), el DERECHO de los pueblos a existir y vivir en paz y la preservación del medio ambiente.

Santiago de Chile, Octubre 2010

Luis Arias Manzo
Fundador—Presidente Mundial
Movimiento Poetas del Mundo
TEL: 633 1200—CEL: 90*5 4212

Culture

International writers converge in Malta for three days of literature, film and music

Vulnerable to the wonder

Adrian Grima

Fahredin Shehu ~ Maelstrom

Fahredin Shehu ~ Maelstrom

Official Sponsor

World Healing ~ World Peace Poetry ~ 2014
www.worldhealingworldpeacepoetry.com

Inner Child Press

Inner Child Press is a Publishing Company Founded and Operated by Writers. Our personal publishing experiences provides us an intimate understanding of the sometimes daunting challenges Writers, New and Seasoned may face in the Business of Publishing and Marketing their Creative "Written Work".

For more Information

Inner Child Press

www.innerchildpress.com

intouch@innerchildpress.com

www.ingramcontent.com/pod-product-compliance
Lightning Source LLC
Chambersburg PA
CBHW070813100426
42742CB00012B/2352